Danger at Sea

Andy and Jill were going to stay with [Gran] and Gramps at the seaside. They we[nt by] train.

'I'm going to build the biggest sandcastle ever,' said Andy.

'And I'm going to spend all my time swimming,' said Jill.

'You'll have to be careful,' said Mum. 'The sea can be very dangerous where Gran and Gramps live.'

Jill couldn't wait to get to the beach. On the first morning of the holiday she was ready to go, long before Gramps had finished his breakfast.

'Come on, Gramps! Hurry up!' said Jill.

'Slow down!' laughed Gramps, 'I'm not as young as I used to be.'

'I'm afraid there'll be no swimming just yet,' said Gran. 'The red flag is flying. That means it's too dangerous to swim in the sea. Look at the size of those waves. They're enormous!'

'Oh no!' groaned Jill. 'Now I think it's starting to rain.'

'How about going to the amusement arcade instead?' asked Gramps.

'Oh yes!' cried Andy and Jill together. 'May we go on the dodgems?'

'Yes, I should think so,' laughed Gran.

The amusement arcade was full of slot machines, but there were dodgems as well. Gramps paid for two cars. Jill and Gran got into one and Andy and Gramps got into the other. A starting bell sounded and the cars began to move.

The cars were all supposed to be going in the same direction but one car, driven by a boy, turned and started to go in the opposite direction. Crash! Andy's car was hit. The boy kept crashing into Andy and Gramps's car making it spin round.

'Hey you! Stop that! Can't you read the notice?' shouted the lady in charge. The boy just laughed.

When the ride was finished Andy and Gramps felt a bit sick. When they came out of the arcade the sun was shining again.

'Perhaps we'll be able to go for a swim now,' said Jill.

Gran, Gramps and the children walked back to the beach but the red flag was still flying.

'Let's go and ask the lifeguard when it might be safe,' said Gran.

The lifeguard was a tanned young man in blue shorts and a t-shirt with the word 'Lifeguard' across the front. His name was Jim. 'The sea is not safe for the time being, but when the tide turns, the wind usually drops and it gets calmer,' he said. 'When it's safe again I'll take the red flag down and put up the green one.'

Gran and Gramps sat in deck chairs on the beach. Jill and Andy made a huge castle and dug a moat around it. Andy was just putting some shells on the top of the castle when a boy came rushing down the beach. It was the boy who had been driving the wrong way on the dodgems.

'Hey!' shouted Jill. 'Look out!' But the boy didn't stop. He jumped on the castle then ran down the beach laughing.

'What a naughty boy!' gasped Gran. Andy and Jill looked at the ruined sandcastle. 'What a horrible thing to do!' said Andy.

'Never mind,' said Gran. 'You can build another. Here's some money. Go and buy us all ice-creams.'

The ice-cream shop also sold toys.

'I'd love a kite,' said Jill. 'I'll ask Gramps if I can buy that big red one.'

Soon the kite was darting and bobbing in the wind high over the beach.

'I'm bored,' said Andy. 'Only one person can play with a kite. I think I'd like to play in the rock pools now.'

'So would I,' said Jill. 'But what shall we do with the kite?'

Gran had a good idea. She took the kite and tied it to her deckchair.

'Don't stray too far away, now,' said Gramps. 'You may only play in the rock pools so long as Gran and I can see you from here.'

Andy and Jill took off their shoes and socks and climbed on to the rocks. The children peered down into the rock pool. Among the shiny green seaweed they could see little green crabs, and tiny sea snails and a starfish. The crabs walked sideways when they were touched, and scuttled away under the rocks.

Suddenly Andy cried out, 'Look, that boy is taking our kite!'

'Hey!' shouted Gramps, who had been asleep in the deckchair. 'What do you think you're doing? Leave that kite alone!'

The boy pulled a face at Gramps and ran off. He had a rubber raft under his arm. It was the same boy who had knocked down the sandcastle.

Just then Jim, the lifeguard, walked down the beach. He stopped the boy. He pointed to the rubber raft and then to the red flag. As Jim walked away the boy stuck his tongue out at him.

'What a rude boy!' said Gramps.

'Look, he's coming this way,' said Jill.

The rude boy walked up to the children. 'My name's Mike,' he said. 'The lifeguard says I should apologize for ruining your castle, but I'm not going to. I just wish he'd take the red flag down so I can go for a swim.'

'So do we,' said Andy and Jill, 'but it's too dangerous at the moment.'

'I don't care what Jim says,' said Mike. 'He just wants to spoil our fun. The sea looks calm to me. I'm going to do what I like.'

'Don't be stupid!' said Andy. 'The waves are still very big and the red flag is flying.'

Mike just laughed, 'Coward!' he sneered. He picked up his raft and put it in the sea near the rocks. The raft bobbed up and down as he climbed into it. Then he began to paddle it around with his hands. 'It's great!' he shouted. 'Come on in and have a go.'

At that second, a huge wave broke over the shore. The raft tipped up and Mike fell off. As the wave rolled back, it dragged the boy and the raft with it. 'Help!' screamed Mike in terror.

Mike clung on to the rubber raft but the strong wind and the current were carrying him away from the shore. He was soon out in deep water. 'Help! Help me!' he shouted.

'What can we do?' asked Andy.

'I'll run and tell Jim,' shouted Jill.

Jim looked very worried as he scanned the sea.

'He's too far out for me to reach,' he groaned. 'This is a job for the lifeboat.'

Jim raced off along the beach to a wooden shed where the lifeboat was kept. Minutes later a rocket shot up in the air and exploded with a loud bang.

The inshore rescue boat was rushed down to the sea. It was a big, black rubber boat with a powerful engine. Two men in red and black wet-suits jumped in and the engine roared as it sped away in a cloud of spray.

'Will they be in time to save Mike?' asked Andy.
'Look!' said Jill. 'They've almost reached him!'

By now the raft was just a red speck on the horizon. It seemed ages before the boat reached it. Andy and Jill saw a man lean over and pull Mike into the boat.

'He's got him!' said Andy. 'I can see him with his arm round Mike. The boat's coming back.'

Andy and Jill ran down the beach to the lifeboat house. Everyone was talking excitedly. Mike was standing in the middle of the crowd, wrapped in a blanket. He was crying and shivering.

'You stupid boy!' said one of the lifeboatmen. 'You could easily have been drowned. Didn't you see the red flag? It's not put up there for a joke.'

'I'm sorry,' sobbed Mike.

'You have been very lucky,' said Jim. 'Those little rubber rafts are dangerous and you should never sail one on the sea. The wind blows you away from the shore and a raft sinks quickly if the plug comes out.'

Andy and Jill made friends with Mike. He had had a nasty shock and he promised never to be silly again. They spent most of the holiday swimming or building giant sandcastles. But they never went into the sea when the red flag was flying.

All About Lighthouses

Gales and storms can drive ships into cliffs, or on to rocks. Many ships are wrecked in this way and many lives are lost.

Sailors have to keep their ships away from rocks. It is often hard to see rocks in the dark and this is where lighthouses help. Lighthouses stand on rocks in the sea or on the shore and flash a warning light to sailors to keep clear of the danger.

Early lighthouses

The first warning lights were just big fires on the tops of cliffs. Modern lighthouses are strong and made of steel and concrete.

Very early lighthouses were built by the Romans. By the year AD 400 they had built over 30. One of them was at Dover, another at Boulogne.

In 1782 a man in Switzerland invented the first glass lighthouse lamp. It burned oil. After 1900 gas and electricity were used to light the lamp.

Modern lighthouses

The most important thing about a lighthouse is that it must be easy to see by day or by night.

That is why lighthouses are painted either white or with coloured bands.

Lightvessels

These are little ships with no engine and no sails. They cannot move unless another ship tows them. They are usually held still by anchor in dangerous parts of the sea.

They have a warning light on top of their mast. A crew lives on them to make sure that the light never goes out. It is a dangerous job as they are tossed about by the waves when the sea is rough.

Grace Darling

This is a true story about a brave girl who saved nine lives.

On the lonely Farne Islands, in the north of England, stands the Longstone Lighthouse. The cruel North Sea beats against the rocks and drives many ships to their doom. It was on these islands that Grace Darling grew up.

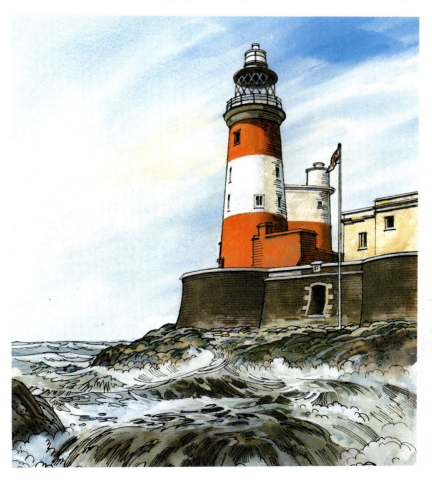

Grace was born in the year 1815. She lived in the lighthouse with her mother and father and eight brothers and sisters.

Grace did not go to school. Her mother taught her to read and write at home. She also learned lots of other useful things like how to trim the oil-lamps in the lantern-room, so that the warning beam never went out. She learned how to row a boat through the dangerous seas round the islands.

On 7th September 1838 Grace woke up very early. There was a terrible storm outside. The sea was crashing against the rocks and the wind was howling around the lighthouse. Grace tossed and turned but she couldn't get back to sleep. 'I hope there are no ships around tonight,' she thought. 'What a terrible storm!'

She got out of bed and climbed up the winding steps to the lantern room to make sure that the light was shining brightly. Grace rubbed the mist off the window and peered out into the dark. Then she gasped! A ship was on the rocks! She dashed downstairs and shook her father awake.

The ship was a paddle steamer called the *Forfarshire*. It was carrying cargo to Scotland, but it also had 39 passengers on board as well as 24 crew members.

That night the ship had had trouble with its engines. The wind and waves drove the ship on to the rocks and a large hole was torn in its side. Water rushed in and the ship started to sink.

A few people managed to get into the ship's lifeboat, but a wave came and washed it away. Suddenly the ship broke in half. Many people fell into the sea and were drowned.

Twelve people were left alive. They managed to scramble on to the slippery rocks close by. The north wind tore at their clothes, and the waves and spray soaked them. Cold and terrified, they clung to the seaweed, waiting for help.

Back at the lighthouse, Mr Darling and Grace peered through their telescope. They could see people clinging to the rocks.

'What can we do?' asked Mr Darling. 'It would be madness to take our wooden rowing boat out in this storm.'

'We must try to reach them. I'll help you to row the boat, I'm very strong,' said Grace.

By now there were only nine people left alive on the rocks. Mr Darling did not want to go, but Grace begged him, and at last he agreed. They launched the boat, Mr Darling took one oar and Grace took the other. They rowed out into the howling storm.

The waves rose so high that their boat was almost swamped. The icy wind cut through their wet clothes. Their fingers went blue with cold. Grace's arms felt like lead. Still they rowed on, until at last they could almost touch the jagged rocks.

The poor people were too scared to let go of the rocks. Mr Darling jumped out through the spray on to the slippery rocks and left Grace alone in the rowing boat. She needed all her strength to keep the heavy boat close to the rocks while, one by one, her father helped four men and one woman to jump into the boat. When the boat was full they turned towards the Longstone Lighthouse and began to row for home.

The trip back took a long time. The storm raged fiercer than ever and the wind lashed Grace and her father. At last they reached the lighthouse where Mrs Darling was waiting with hot drinks and blankets.

There were still four men left on the rocks. Grace was too exhausted to row back so Mr Darling and two men turned the boat round and set out again. A few hours later everyone was safely in the shelter of the lighthouse. The rescue was over.

Most of the ship's crew and passengers were drowned in the storm but Grace and her father had saved nine lives that day. Grace was given silver and gold medals for her bravery. There were stories in the newspapers about her. She did not like all the fuss. The most important thing for her was knowing that she had helped to save nine people from death.